FOLLOWING YOUR DREAM
LIFE OF A PRO SOCCER PLAYER
BEST SOCCER PLAYER OF ALL TIME

By

JERRI WILLIAMS VINCENT

Copyright @2024

All Rights Reserved

ISBN

Hardcover: 978-1-964289-47-2

Paperback: 978-1-964289-16-8

Table of Contents

FORWARD III

    Goals and Dreams: Pathways to Success IV

    Dreams as Motivators V

    The Endless Journey of Life VI

    Dedication of the Book VII

    Special Thanks VIII

CHAPTER ONE – THE LOVE, THE CITY, AND THE MAN WITH A DREAM .... - 1 -

CHAPTER TWO – A FAMILY SPORT .... - 17 -

CHAPTER THREE - ARRIVAL IN BALTIMORE, MARYLAND . - 24 -

CHAPTER FOUR - DREAMS REALIZED .... - 32 -

    The Baltimore Blast Soccer Team .... - 32 -

    The Baltimore Spirit (1992 – 1998) .... - 33 -

    The St. Louis Steamers Soccer Team .... - 34 -

    The Phone Call .... - 34 -

CHAPTER FIVE - COMMUNITY BONDS .... - 36 -

    The Year 1997 .... - 36 -

    Attending My First Soccer Game .... - 37 -

    Attending Another Game with The Baltimore Spirit .... - 38 -

Giving Back to The Community .... - 39 -

CHAPTER SIX - A NEW SOCCER JOURNEY .... - 40 -

Building Bonds in the Community .... - 43 -

Community Engagement in California .... - 45 -

Empowering Others Through Soccer................................ - 46 -

The Boys Group Home Event... - 47 -

Casa Del Sol: A Supportive Community........................... - 48 -

Game Time with the Casa Del Sol Family........................ - 48 -

CHAPTER SEVEN: A LEGACY UNFOLDS .... - 50 -

CHAPTER 8: EMPOWERING THROUGH SOCCER: WOMEN AND GIRLS TAKE THE FIELD .... - 58 -

Acknowledging the Game Changers................................ - 58 -

A Haven for Aspiring Players .... - 59 -

Fostering Holistic Development .... - 59 -

CHAPTER 9: THE BEAUTIFUL GAME'S ENDLESS POSSIBILITIES - 61 -

Empowering Dreams .... - 61 -

Parental Guidance and Support....................................... - 62 -

Smiles, Sportsmanship, and Dreams............................... - 63 -

REFERENCES .... - 66 -

Forward

In the tapestry of life, dreams weave a profound narrative—images, ideas, emotions, and sensations that paint our sleep and consciousness alike. As we delve into the realm of dreams, it's essential to recognize their significance. Dreams, as defined by various sources, encompass a spectrum from psychoanalytic theories to a broader vision of aspirations and goals.

Dreams, however, are not confined to the realms of sleep. They extend beyond, becoming visions, goals, and the driving force behind waking hours. They are the reason we wake up each day, the persistent call to pursue something we could never give up. Success, in the context of dreams, demands determination, courage, and an unwavering passion for the chosen path

Goals and Dreams: Pathways to Success

Goals, the tangible manifestations of dreams, represent desired outcomes, ideal conditions, and long-term aims. They provide direction, understanding, and a framework for personal growth. Attainable and realistic goals empower individuals to navigate challenges, offering a roadmap for personal development.

Ideas of the future, desired results, and personal aspirations define goals. They are the guiding lights, motivating individuals toward meaningful accomplishments. Setting and pursuing these goals is not merely a practical exercise; it is an act of empowerment, a journey that instills motivation and cultivates a sense of purpose.

Dreams as Motivators

In the pursuit of dreams and goals, the concept of daydreams, imagination, and hope plays a crucial role. Tony Stephens, in "True Wealth Starts in The Mind," emphasized the power of mental hygiene—a childhood imagination of going to Disneyland that later manifested into reality. His testimony reflects the potential within each individual to turn dreams into tangible achievements.

As a parent, I harbored dreams for my children—dreams of success, resilience, and the unwavering pursuit of their passions. Being their motivator and supporter meant offering continuous encouragement, reinforcing the belief that their dreams were not only achievable but worth pursuing.

The Endless Journey of Life

Life, like a book with many chapters, unfolds as a journey toward dreams and goals. Turning each page, navigating challenges, and embracing opportunities are integral to the endless possibilities life presents. Empowering children, guiding them through their unique journeys, and teaching them to be great leaders are responsibilities that shape their character and contribute to their success.

Dedication of the Book

This book is dedicated to my son Carlton K. Williams—a testament to his unwavering pursuit of becoming a professional soccer player. His commitment, combined with a well-defined plan, turned dreams into reality. His journey not only inspired his siblings, friends, and family but also served as a beacon of the belief that anything is achievable with determination.

To my daughter, sons, grandchildren, and daughters-in-law, this dedication extends to express gratitude for their unwavering support. Their belief in and support of their oldest brother's dream is a testament to the strength of familial bonds. To my husband and ex-husband and all those who contributed to this journey, your support has been invaluable.

Special Thanks

Special thanks to those who joined me on this journey—my son Carlton Williams, my daughter Tiffany Williams, my son Donald T. Williams, my sisters, my brother, my husband and ex-husband, daughters-in-law, and grandchildren. Your belief and support have made this endeavor possible.

Page Left Blank Intentionally

Chapter One – The Love, The City, and The Man With A Dream

New York City is a place where dreams take shape, where people from all corners of the world converge to seize opportunities, change their lives, and make their wildest dreams come true. My mother, hailing from North Carolina, was one such dreamer. She yearned to uproot her children from their modest beginnings and move them into the bustling heart of New York City. Her vision was to secure a job and offer her children the chance to attend a reputable school. Education was really important for her, and she gave utmost important to us.

And, of course, with such pure intentions, fate smiled upon her very soon as she discovered an opportunity to work at the Manhattan State Psychiatric Hospital, one of the largest psychiatric facilities on the planet, nestled on the island of Manhattan.

This renowned institution was surrounded by water and a smaller islet called Wards Island. On Wards Island stood three towering structures, each soaring 27 floors into the sky. These buildings served a range of purposes, from housing nurses and doctors to offering recreational and rehabilitation services.

The Dunlap Building was a refuge for residents suffering from mental illnesses. Unable to live independently or reintegrate into the community, they received psychiatric treatment, complete with medications and social activity programs. Nurses, physicians, and rehabilitation aides attended to their personal needs, ensuring their safety and well-being. The building's atmosphere buzzed with activities like bingo, knitting, card games, and Pokeno, all designed to foster social interaction and keep residents engaged. Each floor was designated according to where the patients hailed from; for example, those from Harlem resided in "The Harlem Unit."

The Kirby Building mirrored the Dunlap but with an added clinic for patients requiring medical attention. It operated much like a small-scale emergency room.

The Meyer Building, akin to its counterparts, provided similar services. However, it also housed a recreational center boasting pool tables, a bowling alley, a library, and educational programs like GED preparation. Patients could learn valuable skills such as completing housing applications, navigating social security benefits, and using public transportation, all in preparation for their return to the community.

The psychiatric hospital staffed a dedicated team available around the clock, including physicians, nurses, and rehabilitation therapists. Some of the healthcare personnel even resided in a nearby cottage for convenience.

At the heart of my journey, I attended William H. Maxwell High School, an all-female institution in New York City. The school offered a diverse curriculum encompassing general studies, nursing, and cosmetology. Intrigued by the world of beauty, I embarked on a four-year program, learning to treat hair, perform facials and massages, and even dabble in the art of hair coloring and dyeing. Graduating was a significant milestone, but as time went by, my passion for hairstyling waned.

One day, my mother presented me with a new opportunity: a full-time position at the psychiatric hospital. In your teenage years, desires for independence and extra income drive you to explore new horizons. So, from my home in St. Albans, Queens, I journeyed to Manhattan's 125th Street, submitted an application, and within weeks, I received a call from the Human Resources office offering me a job as a Rehab Therapy Aide.

Balancing work at the hospital with my studies at Queensborough College as a full-time student was challenging but fun. It was during this time that I struck up conversations with a man from Trinidad and Tobago, also pursuing higher education at Queens College. Our discussions ranged from our academic work to sports, particularly the beloved New York Knicks basketball team. As our interactions deepened, he began sharing insights on managing the behavior of the hospital's residents when they became agitated or aggressive.

Before I knew it, those conversations evolved into something more profound—love. We embarked on a journey that led to marriage, and in the process, he revealed his childhood dreams, including a burning desire to become a professional soccer player. Soccer had been a significant part of his life in Trinidad, a childhood dream and passion that had never truly faded. As the bustling streets of New York City lay before us, our shared dreams and newfound love would set the stage for a unique journey in the city that never sleeps.

Our Conversations also were over Soccer, a sport that transcends boundaries and cultures, uniting people worldwide through a universal love, passion, and skill. With two teams, the game revolves around a simple yet competitive objective: to drive a ball into the opposing team's goal. This can be achieved by kicking the ball with precision and technique and occasionally by artfully using other parts of the body, excluding, of course, the arms and the hands.

Soccer unfolds on a rectangular field, where the stage is set with netted goals guarding either end. Two teams, driven by ambition and skill, vie for dominance in this arena. Their goal is clear: to score by driving the ball into the opponent's net. This can be accomplished through a variety of techniques, most notably by using any part of the body except the arms and hands. It is a game that celebrates the art of ball control, teamwork, and the sheer exhilaration of a well-executed goal.

In the world of soccer, a team is an orchestra of talent, with each player contributing their unique skills to create harmony on the field. The composition of a soccer team consists of 11 players, one of whom is the goalkeeper, while the remaining 10 are field players. Each player, regardless of their position, shares a common mission: to help their team score goals and prevent the opposing team from doing the same.

The goalkeeper stands as the last line of defense. Their role is distinctive, as they are the sole player authorized to use their arms and hands to protect the goal. However, this privilege is confined to the rectangular penalty area, a space extending 18 yards from each side of the goal.

Defenders form the barricade that safeguards the goalkeeper and the team's goal. Positioned in front of the goalkeeper, their primary responsibility is to thwart the opposition's attempts to score. Among the defenders, the outside fullbacks are the silent sentinels on the right and left flanks, rarely straying from their respective sides of the field.

Central defenders, stationed in the heart of the field, assume the vital task of marking the opposition's most prolific goal scorers, often the center forwards. These defenders are the unsung heroes who protect their team's territory with unwavering dedication.

Center forwards, also known as strikers, are the spearheads of an association soccer team. Their role is to position themselves closest to the opposing team's goal, bearing the primary responsibility for scoring goals. With advanced positions and limited defensive duties, forwards are often the leading goal scorers, lighting up the scoreboard for their team.

Midfielders are the linchpins who connect the dots between defense and attack. Possessing superior physical fitness, they are tasked with covering the most ground during a game. Midfielders must be versatile, capable of penetrating enemy territory during an attack, and seamlessly transitioning to defense when the opposition retains possession.

Forwards, on the other hand, are the architects of goals. Their mission is to fold: to score goals themselves and to create goal-scoring opportunities for their teammates. The center forward, often called a striker, positions themselves in the central area of the opposing team's half, seeking to capitalize on goal-scoring chances.

In soccer, each player contributes a unique note to the symphony of the game, with positions and responsibilities carefully designed to maximize teamwork and strategic play. It is this harmony of roles and responsibilities that makes soccer a truly beautiful sport, where individual brilliance combines with collective effort to create moments of magic on the field.

Soccer's journey through time is a tapestry woven with threads from diverse corners of the world. It was during the early 1800s that soccer took its first steps in the United States within the confines of a North American College Club. In those formative years, it was known as "The Onglides," a name derived from "Oneidas," a group of Native Americans who once inhabited the region around Oneida Lake in central New York.

The Oneida Football Club, founded in Boston, Massachusetts, in 1862, marked a significant milestone in soccer's American journey. It became the pioneering organization to engage in various forms of football within the United States, sowing the seeds of what would become a beloved sport.

While soccer was gaining traction across the Atlantic, it also found its place in the hearts of European countries. The 2nd and 3rd centuries B.C. saw its introduction to China during what historians refer to as the "Han Dynasty Period." The sport became a symbol of unity, with two major periods, the "Western" and

"Eastern" conferences, serving as models for a united empire with a self-perpetuating government.

By the year 1815, soccer had firmly entrenched itself in the culture of universities, colleges, and schools across the United States. It was in 1863 that soccer as we know it today was officially established. Representatives from London clubs convened to form standardized rules for soccer players, a momentous occasion that gave birth to the "Football Association."

The year 1869 marked a pivotal moment as the Football Association laid the foundation for soccer to spread its wings beyond British shores. The game soon found avid enthusiasts among British sailors and, further afield, captivating Italians, Austrians, and Germans who became deeply attached to its allure.

As the 1900s dawned, soccer began to extend its reach to foreign lands, including Italy, Austria, and Germany. Across the ocean in South America, Argentina, Uruguay, and Brazil embraced the sport, making it an integral part of their culture. The establishment of the Federation International de Football Association (FIFA) paved the way for different soccer leagues to organize the inaugural "First World Cup."

The World Cup, an international association football (soccer) competition contested by senior men's national teams, became the pinnacle of the sport, governed by FIFA, the sport's global governing body. The fervor and enthusiasm for soccer continued to grow, captivating hearts and minds across the world.

In the years that followed, the American Soccer League (ASL) emerged as a prominent force in American sports history. Post-World War I, Thomas Cahill, a football executive from St. Louis, played a pivotal role in establishing the league, which thrived for 12 years. Teams from cities such as New York City, Bethlehem, and Providence flourished, attracting players from around the world and even paving the way for radio broadcasts of soccer matches.

By 1912, the Open Challenge Cup had been established, heralding the era of tournament-style leagues. Some league owners diversified their interests, leading to the formation of the "Eastern Soccer League" in 1928, which continued until 1929.

The North American Soccer League (NASL) emerged as a game-changer in the world of soccer. Its establishment allowed soccer to be televised, reaching thousands of homes. In New York

City, "The New York Cosmos" emerged as a powerhouse, attracting one of the world's most renowned soccer players, Pelé.

Pelé, hailing from Brazil, had achieved legendary status with Santos FC. His retirement marked a new chapter in his career, with a lucrative 3-year contract that paid him over 4 million dollars. Pelé's presence was not only felt on the field but also off it, as he engaged with fans by signing autographs and distributing Burger King coupons to boost attendance at soccer games.

A teenage prodigy, Pelé had started playing for Santos at the tender age of 15 and represented the Brazil National Team at 16. His illustrious career included three FIFA World Cup victories and a staggering 77 goals in 92 games. Since his retirement in 1977, he transitioned into an ambassador for football/soccer and even explored acting opportunities.

In 2010, Pelé was bestowed with the honor of being named the Honorary President of the New York Cosmos. His incredible achievements in the sport earned him a place in the Guinness World Record as the most successful domestic league goal scorer. Pelé's legacy, both as a player and a global ambassador for soccer, continues to inspire generations of enthusiasts worldwide.

Therefore, we see how, in the world of sports, countless dreamers emerge from the ranks of young enthusiasts, driven by the hope of someday making it big in their chosen discipline. My ex-husband was one such dreamer whose passion for soccer began as a young boy growing up in the picturesque Caribbean nation of Trinidad and Tobago. This dual-island paradise, nestled near Venezuela, was renowned for its vibrant culture, with Trinidad serving as the capital, notably Port of Spain. Here, the country reveled in the rhythms of calypso music, the splendor of carnival festivals, and the breathtaking beauty of its beaches. However, there was one pursuit that captured the hearts of many—a sport known as soccer.

In Trinidad, the sport bore different monikers, from cricket to football, but in the United States, it was referred to as soccer. In the sun-kissed streets and neighborhoods of Trinidad, children would eagerly grab their black-and-white round balls and kick them around the yard. It was a universal language of joy, a means of interaction, a source of fun, and an activity shared after the school day ended. As the sun dipped below the horizon, casting its golden glow upon the island, children would continue their soccer exploits or gather around television sets and radios to immerse themselves in the game.

Among the stories that fueled their soccer dreams, one name resonated above all others—Pele, the world-famous Brazilian soccer player. My ex-husband's childhood was colored by tales of Pele's exploits on the field, and the excitement was palpable when they learned about this legendary figure who had left an indelible mark on the sport.

As my ex-husband's family made the transition to the United States, the flame of his passion for soccer continued to burn brightly. It was during this time that our paths converged at a psychiatric hospital where we both worked. I was deeply immersed in the world of basketball while he was unwavering in his commitment to soccer. Our conversations often gravitated toward his favorite sport as he shared his fervor and his dream of witnessing Pele in action. Beyond the allure of watching, he nurtured ambitions of playing soccer professionally and someday coaching different soccer teams.

I vividly recall the day when the New York Cosmos Soccer team was slated to play a game on Wards Island, and the legendary

Pele was set to take the field. At that time, I was admittedly unaware of Pele's global stature. However, my ex-husband extended an invitation to the game, which I accepted with intrigue. Little did I know that this event would be an eye-opening experience, not just for me but for the entire crowd in attendance.

As Pele graced the field with his presence, the atmosphere crackled with anticipation. I observed the expressions on the faces of my ex-husband and the surrounding crowd—an amalgamation of joy, wonder, and pure excitement. Laughter echoed, and cheers reverberated through the stadium as Pele showcased his unmatched talent. The New York Cosmos, led by Pele, emerged victorious, etching the memory of that historic game into our hearts.

My ex-husband's journey in pursuit of soccer continued, charting its own unique course. However, it was his decision to join the military services of the Army branch that would mark a significant turning point. Overseas tours became part of his reality, but upon returning to the United States, a new set of orders awaited him. Texas beckoned, and from there, he was directed to report to Lawton, Oklahoma, where he was assigned to Fort Sill's Reynolds Army Hospital.

Even amid the duties and responsibilities of military service, my ex-husband's love for soccer remained unwavering. At Fort Sill, he continued to play for the military team, sharing his expertise and passion by coaching soccer teams and instilling the same love for the game in his two sons. The beautiful game had woven itself into the fabric of his life, leaving an indelible mark on his journey.

Chapter Two – A Family Sport

My son's journey into the world of soccer began even before he could utter his first words. In our family, it was clear from day one that he was destined to have a ball at his feet. While most infants clutched toy rattles, he held onto a round soccer ball, a sign of the passion that would soon consume his life.

As he lay in his crib, tiny hands could be seen pushing that ball around, a prelude to the dribbling skills he would later hone. As he grew and began to crawl, larger soccer balls filled our living room, and he eagerly rolled them around on the floor. Eventually, he graduated to standing, using the living room table for support as he pushed the ball back and forth, displaying an early sense of control and coordination.

When he took his first steps, his father ensured there was always a ball nearby. Our apartment became a miniature soccer pitch, where father and son would kick the ball to each other with infectious enthusiasm. The park became another arena for their playtime, with father and son sharing the joy of passing the ball under the sun.

Years later, as our family expanded to include a second son, the tradition continued. The newborn was introduced to the same spherical companion, holding a ball in his tiny hands and finding comfort in its presence. As he transitioned to crawling, a soccer ball became his loyal sidekick, and soon, he was kicking a miniature ball around the apartment. The brothers, guided by their father's love for the sport, discovered the joy of playing and bonding through their shared passion.

What was truly remarkable was the absence of sibling rivalry. These two brothers never engaged in arguments or negativity toward each other. Instead, their connection was solidified through their shared love for the beautiful game. Whether they were at home, the park, or even the Bronx Zoo, where I ensured we always carried a ball, their playtime was marked by laughter and camaraderie.

Our time in Oklahoma brought new opportunities for their soccer journey. They attended B.C. Swinney School, which offered various athletic programs as part of its curriculum. The school year had distinct seasons for different sports—baseball in the summer, basketball in the winter, fall belonged to the Boy Scouts, and soccer took center stage in the summer.

Both Carlton and Timothy eagerly enrolled in these school activities each year. Witnessing my sons on the field was a source of immense pride and joy. As their mother, I played a supportive role, shuttling them to practice, cheering from the sidelines during games, and ensuring they were well-hydrated with water and a supply of oranges. Their father, on the other hand, was actively involved in their soccer journey, imparting his knowledge of the game, offering encouragement, and teaching valuable lessons on and off the field.

Our Oklahoma home boasted a spacious backyard that extended into a park with swings and sliding boards. This became a hub for their school teammates, who would often come over for impromptu practice sessions. I would prepare sandwiches, oranges, and refreshments for the energetic young players. Saturdays were especially enjoyable because, when some parents had work commitments, they entrusted their children to our care.

In those days, we didn't charge a fee for babysitting. We operated on a principle of community support and care. Parents trusted one another, knowing their children were safe and well looked after. The kids relished the days when their father would step onto the field with them, kicking soccer balls and imparting wisdom about the game's techniques and fundamentals. He encouraged them to embrace the essence of soccer—to have fun and play with unbridled passion.

When we first arrived in Oklahoma, we only had one car, which meant that there was only a single way to get the boys to soccer practice. It was quite chaotic, to say the least, and a typical day would be the boys coming home from school, and off we would go to soccer practice. First, I would have to drop my eldest son to practice and then drop my youngest son to practice. Once that was done, I had to go pick up my ex-husband from Fort Sill Army Base, whereafter I would drop him off at soccer practice, and by the time everyone got dropped, it was time to pick them back up from their individual practices and make them all dinner. And so, by now, you may start to see that this family and their days breathed and lived the game of soccer.

On Saturdays, it would be game time, when my boys and my ex-husband would go to play their games against other teams.

Now, that was an event in itself. We would have to get up very early in the morning and reach the fields by 7 AM. Normally, I would be the one to bring in water, oranges, and food for everyone, but sometimes the parents would all take turns bringing in these items.

My daughter would sit beside me through these games, and we would watch them together. The soccer field became our natural habitat, and we were there from early in the morning to late in the evening. Now, even though I was not playing the sport myself, some might suggest that I was just as closely connected to it as everyone else. I was their coach when they needed motivation, the obsessive audience member to applaud for them; I was their driver and their waterboy alongside, of course, being a mother and a wife.

But as exhilarating as it was, these were the most enjoyable moments. We had the most fun together and the matches would be so entertaining. I absolutely loved watching my children do what they loved, and be amazing at it. Also, it was just an amazing opportunity overall to socialize, as all the parents would be there, alongside teammates and the atmosphere would be exciting, filled with screams and applause.

Sometimes, I would take my boys to a place called "Shaky Pizza," and it was a place that served pizzas, sodas, salads, and many types of food. We would all go in after an exhausting game, and Shaky's Pizza was our retreat. In some instances, their teammates and their families would also join us in this retreat. The families all got together as well through the sport, and alongside the school coach, we would even go to buy uniforms, trophies, and other soccer accessories. We also carpooled on some occasions, and it was the most delightful occasion. You would instantly feel close to the sport, even if you were not into soccer, as the field, its players, and its audience all radiated a strong passion.

Of course, part of the game was losing, too, and the team did have some. The boys would get a little disappointed, but what I loved was that they continued to give their all to each and every game. The main objective was never to win but to stay consistent, motivated, and never give up. They continued to pursue the sport and gave in the work that was required of them.

In life, there would always be a loss following every win, and a win following every loss. These outcomes did not tell of our fate, but merely stood as open doors of oppurtunities. I always taught this to my children, and I made sure they knew that their parents would alwyas be on their side, no matter the path they chose; they would always have our support, always, always have our love.

Chapter Three - Arrival in Baltimore, Maryland

The decision to move to Baltimore, Maryland, marked a significant chapter in our lives. My family had already settled there, drawn by the promise of retirement and the comfort of family support. With several uncles, aunts, and cousins living in Maryland, it was a haven of familiarity, and my mother's presence in the city was especially comforting.

However, when my family embarked on this journey to Baltimore, I remained in Lawton, Oklahoma. It was during this time that my relationship with my ex-husband began to unravel. We found ourselves drifting apart, our paths diverging in ways we hadn't anticipated. This difficult period made me realize the importance of family support, which I desperately needed during these challenging times.

Eventually, the weight of these circumstances led me to make a crucial decision: I needed to relocate my children to Baltimore, Maryland, where they could have the stability and moral support that the family provides. But before making this life-altering move, I took the step of filing for a divorce, acknowledging that our paths had grown too distant to walk together.

Upon my arrival in Baltimore, Maryland, I was welcomed with open arms by my family. I initially stayed at my sister's apartment while I searched for employment and a place to call our own. The kids started attending school, and I wasted no time in my job search. I eventually secured a position at "Church Home Hospital" as a unit secretary, also known as a unit clerk.

In my role as a unit clerk, I was responsible for various tasks, including admitting patients, discharge planning, transcribing physician orders, and preparing patients for surgery. This job allowed me to get back on my feet, and I later transitioned to working as a Certified Nursing Assistant at Mercy Hospital. This move allowed us to relocate to an apartment on the east side of town, closer to where my mother resided. My children also transferred to new schools, Herrin Run High School and Frankford Elementary Middle School.

After school, the boys were eager to continue their soccer journey and engage with their peers. I enrolled them in the Radack Recreation Center, a local facility just a few blocks from our home. The center featured an open soccer field, a playground, basketball courts, and various indoor games and activities. The boys would often head there after completing their homework, staying active, and making friends.

As the school year progressed, I learned about DE Burns Arena in Canton, Maryland, a versatile indoor sports and entertainment facility. It was named after an African American Mayor of Baltimore City. Excited about the opportunity, my sons joined the indoor soccer league hosted at this arena. While I was at work in the hospital, they would meet me in front of the hospital, and together, we'd take the bus to the arena.

Later, when my mother found out about the distance we were traveling to support her grandsons' soccer pursuits, she insisted that my stepdad take us to the games. Her enthusiasm for her grandsons' soccer endeavors was heartwarming, and it led her to attend some of their games. I couldn't have been prouder of her involvement, as it symbolized the reconnection and support of my extended family, which had been challenging due to the nomadic military lifestyle we previously lived. It was a heartwarming reunion and a reminder of the power of family support during life's transitions.

After some years living in Baltimore, it was time for me to allow the kids to relocate back to Oklahoma with their dad due to what was in the divorce papers. It was somewhat difficult to explain to the kids that they were going back to Oklahoma, but they were supportive and really were not adapted to the lifestyle of living in an urban city. There became some issues with the schools, such as kids wanting to bully my middle son, and my oldest son's grades weren't being reported on his report card due to the lack of teachers at the school. So, I did become a little fearful that the boys would be harmed and not safe living in Baltimore, Maryland, but the love was always and still is there.

When my sons returned to Oklahoma, they continued their school careers by attending MacArthur Middle and High School. They enrolled in the school activity sport of soccer, and they both continued to have their father's support in coaching them in the game of soccer. They enjoyed playing on the fields against other teams, taking hits, enduring falls, facing losses, and celebrating wins. They never gave up. Alongside their studies in school, they attended church on Sundays, helped with chores around the house, and even cared for their baby sister.

Both of my sons were not only players but also mentors to their teammates. In the end, it was all about team spirit and unity as a family because the soccer team members became their extended family. They never gave up on each other and had a deep brotherly love.

My oldest son, Carlton, continued high school in Lawton, Oklahoma, at MacArthur High School. It was the third high school built in Lawton, Oklahoma, and had a strong soccer program. He continued to excel academically, always emphasizing the importance of education. During his last year, talent scouts from various universities visited his school games, hoping to recruit promising players. Carlton's dedication paid off when he was recruited to Oklahoma Christian University on a full scholarship.

During his studies at the university, Oklahoma City was hit by a domestic bombing terrorist attack that targeted the Alfred P. Murrah Federal Building in downtown Oklahoma City on April 19, 1995. I was terrified for Carlton's safety, but he assured me that the university was not directly affected. The incident left a lasting impact on the city, but the students and teachers were unharmed. This was a reminder of the importance of keeping faith and staying strong during challenging times.

Carlton continued to excel at Oklahoma Christian University, catching the attention of scouts and coaches from other universities, one of which was the University of South Florida in Tampa, Florida. Carlton decided to transfer to the University of South Florida to further his soccer career.

Relocating to Florida presented an exciting opportunity for Carlton to gain exposure in the world of soccer. His friend from MacArthur High School also had the same opportunity, but due to limited funds, they had to take turns. Carlton's success and the opportunities that came his way made me incredibly proud.

Carlton's passion for soccer led him to become a coach. He obtained coaching licenses from the United Soccer Federation and a Coerver Coaching Diploma, which deepened his understanding of the game and prepared him to share his knowledge with others. He started by volunteering at recreational centers, working with kids, and teaching them the sport he loved.

His coaching journey continued as he mentored players of all ages, including all-girls' and boys' soccer teams. Carlton's approach to coaching was about having fun and fostering a love for the game.

While studying at the University of South Florida, Carlton had an unexpected opportunity to star in a movie. Producers spotted him on the soccer field and asked if he was interested in trying out for a role in the film "The Waterbody," starring Adam Sandler and Laurence Gillard Jr.

Carlton was thrilled to accept the role of the soccer kicker in the movie. His excitement was contagious, and I could hear it in his voice when he called to share the news. It was a dream come true to be part of a major Hollywood production.

As the soccer kicker in "The Waterbody," Carlton had the chance to work alongside Laurence Gillard Jr. His role in the movie was a significant achievement, and I was overjoyed to see my son on the big screen. Carlton's experience taught us both the importance of seizing opportunities when they come your way.

His success in both soccer and the film industry was a testament to his determination, passion, and hard work. Carlton's journey from returning to Oklahoma to pursuing his dreams and achieving success was a story of resilience and perseverance.

Chapter Four - Dreams Realized

The Baltimore Blast Soccer Team

The Baltimore Blast Soccer team had a storied history in Charm City. Founded by North Carolina-based software executive Bill Stealey, the team initially joined the Major Indoor Soccer League (MISL) and quickly became a beloved part of Baltimore's sports scene in the 1980s. Their bright red, orange, and yellow uniforms matched the team's aggressive style on the soccer field.

The Baltimore Blast played their first home game at the Civic Center in downtown Baltimore in November 1980. Under the leadership of head coach Kenny Cooper, they posted a 21-19 record in their inaugural season. They were known for their pre-game ceremonies, emerging from a giant neon soccer ball suspended from the arena's ceiling, creating a captivating atmosphere.

The Blast's players worked tirelessly to win games and bring championship trophies to Baltimore. The bonds they formed with the fans were deep, and they cherished the community's support.

On June 8, 1984, before a record crowd of 12,000 loyal fans, the Blast won their first MISL title, defeating the St. Louis Steamers. The following season, the team experienced its first ownership change when local businessman Ed Hale acquired the Blast.

In 1991-1992, local businessperson Cooper joined forces to launch "The Baltimore Spirit," a National Professional Soccer League franchise. In 1997-1998, Ed Hale regained ownership and changed the team's name back to the "Baltimore Blast."

The Baltimore Spirit (1992 – 1998)

The Baltimore Spirit, a professional soccer team in the National Professional Soccer League (NPSL), emerged in 1992 after the MISL folded. Founded by J.W. "Wild Bill" Stealey, a software executive, and longtime Baltimore Blast season ticket holder, the Spirit aimed to keep indoor soccer thriving in Baltimore.

The Baltimore Spirit played their home games at the Baltimore Arena, sharing the space with other sports teams like the Baltimore Skipjacks and the Baltimore Bandits. This marked a new chapter in Baltimore's soccer history.

The St. Louis Steamers Soccer Team

The original St. Louis Steamers, which played in the Major League Indoor Soccer League from 1974 to 1988, was a popular team known for its passionate fan base. Their average attendance exceeded 12,000 during the early 1980s, even surpassing the NHL's St. Louis Blues in attendance for several seasons.

After a brief hiatus, indoor soccer returned to St. Louis with the St. Louis Storm from 1989 to 1992. The Storm led the MISL in attendance in 1991 and 1992.

One month after the MISL folded in July 1992, Dr. Abraham Hawatmer purchased the Tulsa Ambush of the NPSL. He hired former Steamers and Storm favorite Daryl Doran as a player for the team.

The Phone Call

Receiving that phone call from my son was a moment of pure joy. He excitedly shared the news that he was returning to

Baltimore to play for the Baltimore Blast Soccer team. The dream had come true, and he was now a professional soccer player. Tears welled up in my eyes as I listened to his voice filled with happiness.

My son explained that he and his friend Mike had both been picked up by the team, and they needed a place to stay. I didn't hesitate to agree and offered my boyfriend's newly purchased three-bedroom home on the east side of town. It was spacious enough to accommodate all of us.

The excitement of seeing my son's dreams come true was overwhelming. I had grown up as a basketball fan, attending New York Knicks games at Madison Square Garden. Little did I know that years later, my own son would have the opportunity to play in Baltimore's Convention Center, just as I had watched the Knicks play in Maryland. Dreams were indeed being realized, and I couldn't have been prouder.

Chapter Five - Community Bonds

The Year 1997

In the year 1997, Carlton's call brought news that filled my heart with an overwhelming joy. He excitedly shared that he had been selected to play for the Baltimore Spirit Team. Jumping up and down, I couldn't contain my happiness. A call to my family followed, spreading the news of Carlton's return to Baltimore. The collective screams of joy echoed through the phone lines as my mother, sisters, and brother shared in the pride of Carlton's achievement.

When Carlton arrived in Maryland, it was a true homecoming celebration. Hugs, kisses, and love filled the air, and he brought along his teammate, Mike. The first request from my son was a classic home-cooked meal featuring fried chicken and my famous potato salad.

After picking them up from the bus station, we gathered at home for a hearty meal and conversations that echoed with laughter. The next morning, before the sun had risen, the boys were outside, ready for their morning routine of running, push-ups, and sit-ups. Their dedication to physical exercise showcased the discipline required for professional soccer.

The Convention Center became their daily hub, where they met their coach, signed contracts, and prepared for the upcoming season. Excitement filled their voices as they shared the details of joining a professional soccer league, getting a salary, and having the opportunity to showcase their talents to thousands of fans.

For the first few weeks, the boys stayed with us before moving into their own apartment. The experience of independence, driving to practice together, sharing meals, and supporting each other formed lasting bonds among the teammates.

Attending My First Soccer Game

The thrill of watching my son play his first professional game in front of thousands was indescribable. Carlton surprised me with tickets, and the anticipation leading up to the game brought tears of joy to my eyes. Accompanied by my boyfriend, we entered the arena, immersed in the atmosphere of lights, concession stands, and the hum of excited fans.

Locating our seats, the countdown to game time began. As the Baltimore Blast players were announced, the crowd erupted with cheers. The energy was contagious, and my heart swelled with pride as Carlton's name echoed through the arena.

Attending Another Game with The Baltimore Spirit

Another game day, another wave of excitement. Driving through the bustling streets of Baltimore, we reached the Convention Center. The venue, with its vast space and various amenities, was a testament to the growing popularity of soccer in the city.

The arena was a sea of red and gold as fans proudly displayed their Baltimore Spirit gear. The game unfolded with electrifying energy, each kick and pass drawing roars from the crowd. The Baltimore Spirit players, including my son Carlton, showcased their skills with finesse and determination.

The experience of attending soccer games became a regular joy. The cheering, the camaraderie, and the pride of seeing Carlton pursue his passion were moments etched in my memory.

Giving Back to The Community

Beyond the thrill of the games, the Baltimore Spirit team embraced a commitment to giving back to the community. Carlton and his teammates actively participated in community events, engaging with neighbors through food, games, and entertainment.

Hospital visits, community events, and school sponsorships became integral parts of the team's outreach. Carlton expressed the joy he felt in putting a smile on others' faces, especially children who attended soccer games.

The team's dedication to community service reinforced the idea that success on the field should be accompanied by a sense of responsibility to uplift the community that supports them. Carlton's words echoed the sentiment, "I enjoy seeing them smile, and that's what makes me happy." The Baltimore Spirit wasn't just a team on the field; it was a source of inspiration and joy for the entire community.

Chapter Six - A New Soccer Journey

The Baltimore Spirit Soccer team had created countless memories at the Baltimore Arena, but as contracts have their timelines, Carlton's tenure with the team was coming to an end. As the final days approached, a new opportunity emerged. The St. Louis Ambush Soccer Team, based in Missouri, extended an invitation to Carlton to join their ranks.

The St. Louis Ambush, a professional indoor soccer team, had roots in Tulsa before finding its home in St. Louis. Established in 1991, the team dissolved in 2000. The games were hosted at the St. Louis Arena and the Kiel Center, with Dr. Abraham Hawatmel and Richard Rende as the team's owners. Being part of the National Premier Soccer League (NPSL), the St. Louis Ambush had a significant presence in the soccer scene.

In an interesting turn, the team had undergone a name change. Once known as the St. Louis Ambush, they later adopted the moniker St. Louis Steamers when they joined the Major Indoor Soccer League (MISL). The switch to the St. Louis Steamers brought increased popularity, especially during the 1981-1982 game season.

Despite facing challenges and financial discord, the St. Louis Steamers persevered. The team eventually folded, but the MISL returned to the city with the same name. After the MISL folded in July 1992, the owners brought back former coach Daryl Doran.

In the years that followed, the St. Louis Steamers Arena expanded with the opening of the Kiel Arena in 1995-1996, providing a larger facility for an ever-growing fan base (funwhilelasted.net).

With this backdrop, Carlton received an enticing offer from the St. Louis Ambush Soccer team. The coach's call marked the beginning of a new chapter. Packing his belongings and bidding farewell to his former teammates in Baltimore, he set out on a journey to St. Louis, Missouri.

Before departing, Carlton visited me, and we shared cherished moments over a meal of fried chicken and potato salad. The conversation revolved around staying safe, giving his best on the field, staying coachable, focused, and spiritual – all while relishing the joy that soccer brought into his life.

Upon his arrival in St. Louis, Carlton was welcomed by his new teammates. The camaraderie flowed through conversations about soccer experiences, past teams, and aspirations for the St. Louis Ambush/St. Louis Steamers. Evenings were spent bonding over dinner, watching television, and Carlton diligently adhering to his nightly exercise routine.

The official induction into the team happened the next day at the arena. The coach outlined team expectations, introduced Carlton to his new teammates, and then came the moment of pride – receiving the teal, white, and black team jersey with the number 16 and his name, Williams, proudly displayed.

As Carlton settled into the city and embraced his role with the St. Louis Ambush, excitement permeated his voice. While I couldn't witness his games in Missouri, the opportunity arose when the team played against West Coast teams in Sacramento. The journey with the St. Louis Ambush marked a new chapter in Carlton's soccer career, filled with anticipation, challenges, and the promise of creating more unforgettable moments on the field.

Building Bonds in the Community

Carlton's journey in California extended beyond the soccer field as he actively engaged with the local community. After settling in Manteca, California, Carlton reached out to inform me about his upcoming games against various soccer teams. Overwhelmed with joy, I decided to organize a surprise reunion with his sister, who hadn't seen him in five years.

In preparation for the surprise, I invited all my co-workers from The Older Adult Day Treatment Program in Stockton, California, along with my in-laws. The surprise unfolded at the Arco Arena in Sacramento, California, where Carlton was playing. Greeted with love, hugs, and kisses, Carlton, as always, expressed his desire for his favorite meal – potato salad and fried chicken.

The arena buzzed with excitement as game time approached. The dimming lights and pulsating music heightened the anticipation as both teams were introduced. When Carlton's name was called, the cheers erupted. Amidst the fervor, a spectator approached me, questioning why I was cheering for Carlton instead of the Sacramento team. Politely, I revealed that Carlton was my son, and the spectator, in turn, extended his congratulations.

The national anthem marked the beginning of the game, and the action unfolded. Carlton showcased his skills, using his chest to control the ball, expertly kicking it to teammates, and tirelessly preventing the opposing team from scoring. As the game concluded, Carlton joined the coach and players for post-game discussions.

After the game, Carlton made his way to the stands to meet me, where I revealed the surprise presence of his sister. The emotional reunion added a special touch to the day. Carlton also took the time to meet my co-workers, in-laws, and fans, signing autographs and posing for pictures.

This event sparked a tradition. Carlton continued to invite family, co-workers, and even residents from Casa Del Sol, an assisted living home in Stockton, to his games. We formed a vibrant and supportive group, creating posters, wearing personalized T-shirts, and adorning ourselves with soccer-themed jewelry. The ritual of cheering Carlton on after each game, getting autographs, and capturing memorable moments became a shared joy.

Community Engagement in California

As Carlton's career flourished, he remained committed to giving back to the community. Three significant events highlighted his dedication.

Older Adult Day Treatment Center: Carlton visited the Older Adult Day Treatment Center, providing a haven for individuals diagnosed with depression. His presence offered inspiration and an opportunity for the clients to interact with a successful athlete. Carlton's career became a source of motivation and conversation, fostering connections between generations.

Stockton Senior Center: The Stockton Senior Center welcomed Carlton during one of their Bingo Days. Carlton actively engaged with the seniors, assisting them with the game and serving snacks. His genuine interactions, assistance, and willingness to be part of their activities left a lasting impression on the seniors and staff.

All-Boys Group Home: Carlton extended his outreach to an all-boys group home, creating a positive impact on the lives of young individuals. By sharing his journey and experiences, he became a mentor figure, offering guidance and inspiration to those navigating their own paths.

These community events became integral to Carlton's mission of connecting with people, fostering a sense of belonging, and inspiring others to pursue their dreams. As he continued to make a mark on the soccer field, Carlton's off-field contributions echoed the importance of community, support, and shared joy in the pursuit of success.

Empowering Others Through Soccer

The culmination of community events reached its pinnacle at Casa Del Sol, a family-owned assisted living home in Stockton, California. This facility provided services to individuals diagnosed with depression, offering assistance with daily activities, medication monitoring, and support for doctor appointments. Residents could also attend the "Older Adult Day

Treatment Center" for various therapies and engage in community events.

The Boys Group Home Event

The owner of Casa Del Sol, an advocate deeply rooted in community programs, orchestrated an event at an all-boys group home. This initiative aimed to provide support and inspiration to young individuals facing trauma and mental health challenges. Carlton, as the guest speaker, shared his journey from a young kid learning soccer from his father to playing professionally and eventually coaching and mentoring others.

During the Q & A session, Carlton emphasized the importance of enjoying the game, addressed handling injuries, and shared motivational words given after losses. However, the most emotional moment came when Carlton expressed how seeing his mother in the crowd motivated him to play. This revelation touched hearts and resonated with the audience.

The event concluded with pictures, autographs, and interactions, leaving a lasting impact on both Carlton and the boys at the group home. Carlton expressed that it was one of the best events he had attended, reinforcing the power of connecting with and inspiring others.

Casa Del Sol: A Supportive Community

Casa Del Sol, nestled in Stockton, California, boasted a diverse staff, including individuals from African American and Mexican cultures. Their dedication went beyond maintaining the facility; they actively engaged residents in daily activities, meals, and festive events. The facility's inclusive atmosphere extended to extraordinary holiday celebrations, cookouts, and musical events.

Game Time with the Casa Del Sol Family

Collaborating with the owner, we organized a soccer game in a local park for the staff. Recognizing the significance of soccer in Mexican and Spanish-speaking communities, we aimed to celebrate Chico DeMaio Day with a match. The event drew participation from co-workers, Carlton's sister, and even spectators from the park's surroundings.

As parents, we trusted our children to spend time together, fostering empowerment and unity. The game was not just about soccer; it symbolized a coming together of diverse backgrounds for a common cause. People passing by stopped to watch, and even those from nearby homes joined the event, creating an impromptu community gathering.

After the game, the atmosphere was filled with joy, laughter, and the shared satisfaction of uniting for a positive cause. The experience highlighted the transformative power of sharing skills and empowering others. The trust between families, the camaraderie among the staff, and the joyful community engagement underscored the importance of collective efforts for the betterment of all.

In summary, the events at Casa Del Sol exemplified the impact that empowering others can have, creating a ripple effect of positivity, unity, and shared joy within the community.

Chapter Seven: A Legacy Unfolds

The transition from player to retiree had ushered in unexpected blessings and opportunities for Carlton, shaping a new chapter in his life's story. As the final whistle blew on his playing career with the St. Louis Soccer team, Carlton found himself at the beginning of a remarkable journey that would not only secure his financial future but also redefine his impact on the sport he held dear.

In the heart of Missouri, fate had a surprise in store for Carlton in the form of a remarkable woman named Christina. Their connection blossomed, leading to a marriage that brought joy not only to the couple but also to their expanding family as two delightful children became the newest additions.

As the years wove their tapestry, Carlton found himself contemplating his retirement and the desire to give back to the game that had given him so much. The idea of soccer camps took root in his mind, driven by a passion for the sport and a belief in the power of individualized training for young players.

Carlton's vision for these camps became a reality with the unwavering support of his wife, Christina. Her business acumen seamlessly complemented his soccer expertise, making them a dynamic team. Carlton focused on the on-field aspects, ensuring top-notch coaching and suitable locations for the camps, while Christina expertly handled the administrative intricacies, financial management, and extensive marketing required to make these camps a success.

The impact of these soccer camps rippled through the local community, catching the attention of the owner of the St. Louis Scott Gallagher Soccer Club. Recognizing Carlton's positive influence, discussions were initiated to integrate his successful camps with the esteemed soccer club. The proposal extended an enticing offer – a position as the Director of Soccer.

Accepting the role meant more than overseeing the camps; it meant contributing to the development of the club's programs and fostering a culture of excellence. The St. Louis Scott Gallagher Soccer Club, with its rich history and commitment to player development, provided Carlton with an opportunity to continue shaping the soccer landscape in the Greater St. Louis Metropolitan Area.

As the Director of Soccer, Carlton brought his wealth of experience, passion, and dedication to the club. The union of his successful soccer camps with the esteemed institution promised a bright future for aspiring young players in the community. The collaboration wasn't just a professional commitment; it was a platform for Carlton to continue shaping the future of soccer, one goal at a time.

Little did Carlton know that this new chapter would evolve into a journey of mentorship, development, and community impact. The St. Louis Scott Gallagher Soccer Club became more than a club; it became a conduit for Carlton to leave an indelible mark on the soccer world, solidifying his legacy as a driving force behind the sport's growth and nurturing the dreams of young players who aspired to follow in his footsteps.

As Carlton settled into his role as the Director of Soccer at the St. Louis Scott Gallagher Soccer Club, he reflected on the journey that had brought him to this point. The phone call from the club's owner had been a pivotal moment, filling him with a mix of excitement and gratitude. The meeting that followed was not just an offer of a position; it was an affirmation of his lifelong dedication to the beautiful game.

For Carlton, coaching was more than a profession; it was a passion that had deep roots in his earlier experiences at the St. Louis Gallagher Community Center. The introduction of soccer for girls had left a lasting impression on him, and now, as the Director of Soccer, he found himself presented with the opportunity to coach an all-girls soccer team—a prospect that thrilled him.

The St. Louis Scott Gallagher Soccer Club, formerly known as the Busch Gardens Soccer Club, had a rich history dating back to the efforts of Dennis Long, a soccer enthusiast and Anheuser-Busch executive. Long's contributions to soccer in St. Louis were significant, including his role in the development of the St. Louis Soccer Park and the establishment of a soccer club for boys.

By the 1980s, the club had evolved into the Busch Soccer Club, expanding to include a girls' team in subsequent years. In 2004, the club underwent a transformation, adopting the name St. Louis Scott Gallagher Soccer Club to better reflect its mission and community focus. The club's commitment to excellence was evident as it consistently ranked among the top soccer programs in the country.

The St. Louis soccer legacy extended beyond the city limits, crossing the Mississippi River into southern Illinois. The growth of the sport in schools and smaller clubs paved the way for the formation of the Metro United Soccer Club. This new club, established in southern Illinois, shared a commitment to professional-level training for boys and girls of all ages and abilities. Working in collaboration with Scott Gallagher SC, Metro United FC aimed to maximize player development and provide a robust soccer experience for the community.

As Carlton delved into the vibrant soccer culture of St. Louis, he realized that his role as Director of Soccer was not just about leading the soccer camps or coaching teams. It was about being part of a broader narrative—a narrative that celebrated the rich history of soccer in the region, embraced the values of community and development, and looked towards a future where the love for the game would continue to flourish, driven by the dedication of individuals like himself and the entire St. Louis Scott Gallagher Soccer Club community.

The year 2007 marked a significant turning point in the soccer landscape of the Greater St. Louis Metropolitan Area. The St. Louis Soccer Club, Scott Gallagher Soccer Club, and Metro United Soccer Club, recognizing the potential for collaboration, entered into a transformative deal. The vision was clear: by merging the strengths, talents, and efforts of these three leading clubs, they aimed to better serve the soccer community and maintain a competitive edge as the sport continued to flourish nationally.

The amalgamation of these powerhouse clubs was more than a consolidation of resources; it was a strategic move to elevate soccer in the region. The collaboration enabled the clubs to pool their expertise, coaching staff, and developmental programs. This synergy aimed not only to enhance the player experience but also to foster a more comprehensive and cohesive soccer community.

With the merger, St. Louis could boast a united front, combining the storied history of each club to create a powerhouse that could compete at the national level. The Greater St. Louis

Metropolitan Area became a hub for soccer excellence, drawing attention from aspiring players, coaches, and enthusiasts alike.

Under the umbrella of this unified soccer entity, the St. Louis Scott Gallagher Soccer Club, with its Director of Soccer, Carlton, played a pivotal role in shaping the collective vision. The collaboration allowed for the continued growth and evolution of soccer programs, ensuring that young players received top-notch training and development opportunities.

The impact of this alliance extended beyond the soccer field. It created a sense of unity and community pride, fostering an environment where players could not only refine their skills but also forge lifelong connections with fellow enthusiasts. The St. Louis soccer community became a beacon for aspiring talents and a model for how collaboration could strengthen the foundations of the sport.

As the three clubs seamlessly integrated their operations, the Greater St. Louis Metropolitan Area witnessed a resurgence in soccer enthusiasm. The combined efforts of the St. Louis Soccer Club, Scott Gallagher Soccer Club, and Metro United Soccer Club laid the groundwork for a soccer renaissance, ensuring that the region remained at the forefront of the sport's growth.

The year 2007, marked by the unification of these clubs, became a symbol of progress, collaboration, and a shared commitment to the beautiful game.

Little did they know that this strategic alliance would not only shape the immediate future of soccer in the area but also leave a lasting legacy, inspiring generations of players, coaches, and soccer enthusiasts in the years to come.

Chapter 8: Empowering Through Soccer: Women and Girls Take the Field

In the evolution of soccer within the United States, a profound shift occurred over the years, challenging traditional perceptions of the sport as solely for boys and men. A pivotal figure in recognizing the need for inclusivity in soccer was the owner of the St. Louis Scott Gallagher Soccer Club.

Acknowledging the Game Changers

For a long time, soccer had been predominantly associated with male players. However, a realization emerged that the sport held equal opportunities for girls and women. The St. Louis Scott Gallagher Community Center emerged as a pivotal institution in fostering this change. Carlton, fueled by his passion for the game and commitment to inclusivity, took up the mantle of coaching girls' teams, becoming a champion for the cause.

A Haven for Aspiring Players

The St. Louis Scott Gallagher Community Center became more than just a soccer facility; it transformed into a haven for girls and women in the community eager to pursue the sport. Carlton, honored to contribute to this transformative journey, coached various girls' teams, including the SLSG Girls Class of 2020 and the SLSG Navy Team.

The community center's significance extended beyond coaching sessions—it became a hub for soccer tournaments. One of the highlights was the SLSG Girls Fall Classic, a massive event that saw the participation of 446 teams in St. Louis, Missouri, reflecting the growing enthusiasm for girls' soccer in the region.

Fostering Holistic Development

The community center wasn't just about soccer; it aimed to cultivate well-rounded individuals. It provided a nurturing environment for academic pursuits alongside athletic endeavors. Girls had the opportunity to not only excel on the field but also attend major soccer events, such as the NCAA Women's College Cup Tournament. This prestigious competition, organized by the National Collegiate Athletic Association, determined the Division 1 women's national champion.

The integration of soccer with academic and professional development underscored the commitment to empowering girls and women through the beautiful game. The community center became a symbol of progress, breaking down barriers and opening doors for countless young female athletes.

As Carlton witnessed the growth of girls' soccer within the community, he understood that this was not just about kicking a ball on the field; it was about breaking stereotypes, fostering dreams, and creating a legacy where every girl felt empowered to take their place on the soccer stage. The St. Louis Scott Gallagher Soccer Club had become a beacon for inclusivity in soccer, demonstrating that the sport was truly for everyone, regardless of gender.

Chapter 9: The Beautiful Game's Endless Possibilities

In retrospect, the evolution of soccer in the United States is a testament to its rise as a major sport, captivating the hearts and minds of enthusiasts across the nation. The surge in popularity is evident in the remarkable average attendance figures, with Major League Soccer securing its place as the eighth most attended league in the world.

From 2013 to 2018, the average MLS attendance stood at 21,358, a commendable feat that places it among the elite, trailing only behind renowned leagues like Ligue 1 in France. The United States, with an average attendance of 60,000, exemplifies the nation's fervor for the sport. Soccer has become a unifying force, opening doors for aspiring players of all ages and genders.

Empowering Dreams

Soccer, once considered an emerging sport, has now become a catalyst for empowerment. It provides a platform for girls and boys, men and women alike, to pursue their dreams, fostering a sense of empowerment and passion for the beautiful game. The journey has been monumental, and the sport continues to inspire the next generation of athletes.

As a parent, witnessing my son's journey in soccer was not only fulfilling but also enlightening. His resilience, coupled with a perpetual smile, showcased the essence of good sportsmanship. Regardless of victory or defeat, he maintained an unwavering commitment to his dream, teaching valuable lessons to his siblings and children.

Parental Guidance and Support

The role of parents and friends in nurturing these dreams cannot be overstated. Becoming a pillar of support, offering encouragement in moments of triumph or adversity, and guiding young athletes through the challenges of their chosen path are invaluable contributions. It is a journey that shapes character, instills discipline, and fuels the pursuit of excellence.

Parental involvement goes beyond the sidelines. It extends to teaching the importance of giving back to the community. Attending extraordinary events, delivering motivational speeches to diverse groups, and networking with social agencies are ways to instill a sense of social responsibility. The impact of such involvement extends far beyond the soccer field.

Smiles, Sportsmanship, and Dreams

Amidst the wins and losses, what mattered most was seeing my son's genuine smile. His embodiment of good sportsmanship, his refusal to succumb to the challenges, and his unyielding commitment to his dreams left an indelible mark. His legacy transcends the boundaries of the soccer field, encouraging others to follow their dreams.

The essence of the message is simple yet profound: Teach your children the importance of pursuing their dreams. Be the coach, motivator, and inspiration they need. Embrace the bumps and falls, and witness the remarkable transformation that occurs when dreams are pursued with dedication and resilience.

In closing, remember that behind every dream lies a world of opportunities waiting to unfold. The beautiful game has not only given my son a career but also a platform to inspire others. As we celebrate the growth of soccer in the United States, let us continue to empower the dreams of future athletes, ensuring that the legacy of passion, sportsmanship, and perseverance lives on.

"Soccer is ballet with a ball," a sentiment shared by Carlton's father, resonates as a reminder that soccer is not just a sport—it is an art form. Carlton embodies this artistry, and his journey serves as an inspiration to all who dare to dream and pursue their passions.

Carlton Williams

REFERENCES

1. Baltimore Blast Soccer Team: https://baltimoreblast.com
2. Baltimore Convention Center- www.bcenter.org
3. B.C. Swinney Elementary School, https://classmates.com
4. Clarence Du burns Recreation Center, https://en.m.wikipedia.org
5. Casa Del Sol Assisted Living Home, https://myelp.com.biz.casa del
6. Co erver Coaching Philosph- https:// wwwcoervesmoves.com
7. Copyright@2019 Baltimore Blast (Soccer Shift) Baltimoreblast.com
8. En.wikipedia.org.wiki
9. Funwhilelasted.net
10. Global Futbal Training , https://www.giftskills.com
11. https:/en.mwikipedia.org.wiki
12. http://www.coervermoves.com
13. http://my-bicyle-andi.co.uk published, June 16, 2013

14. Jump" Take the Leap to Faith to Achieve Your Life Abundance- By Steve Harvey

15. Manhattan State Psychiatric Hospital, Wards Island New York City, (Wikipedia)

16. MacArthur Middle & Hight School, https://www.lawtonps.orgmacarth

17. Mental Health Responding to the Needs of the African American Senior Population 2010 p.p.23 p.3 , Jerri Williams Vincent

18. Movie "The Water Boy " – Adam Sandler, 1998, http://en.m.wikipedia.org>wiki

19. National Professional Soccer League Median Guides

20. National Premier Soccer League (Wikipedia)

21. Radecke Recreation Park, https://parkxamerica.org>radeck

22. Sacramento, California" Arco Arena, https://en.m.wikipedia.org.wiki

23. San Joaquin Mental Health Older Adult Day Treatment Center, Stockton, California

24. https://wjcbhs.org.older_adult

25. Stockton Senior Center- , Stockton, California , http://www.cistockton.ca.us.senior

26. St. Louis Gallagher Soccer Club, https:www.sisgsoccer.com

27. St. Louis Ambush Soccer Team, https://www.stlambush.com

28. Trinidad and Tobago Country In The Caribbean, https://en.m.wikipedia.org.wiki

29. The (APA Dictionary of Psychology), seventh edition

30. "True Wealth Starts in The Mind "– Lisa A. Jones , p.p. 174 p.4, p.p.175 p.1

31. University of Florida, https://www.upl.edu

32. Wikipedia (Thunder of The Lacrosse League)

33. Wikipedia, ccby-SA 3.0

34. www.barleyby.com.essay " How Dreams Lead To Success " , PKHGUG

35. www.bccenter.orgwebsite: Wikipedia

36. Wikipedia>Wiki Baltimore Blast

37. 1980-1981 through 1983-1984 (Wikipedia) NHL's St. Louis Blues

Made in the USA
Columbia, SC
25 June 2024

37455297R10043